Primary Sources in World History

THE MIDDLE AGES

ENZO GEORGE

Cavendish Square
New York

Published in 2017 by Cavendish Square Publishing, LLC
243 5th Avenue, Suite 136 New York, NY 10016

Website: cavendishsq.com

CPSIA compliance information: Batch #CS16CSQ.

Library of Congress Cataloging-in-Publication Data

Names: George, Enzo.
Title: The Middle Ages / Enzo George.
Description: New York : Cavendish Square, 2016. | Series: Primary sources in world history | Includes index.
Identifiers: ISBN 9781502618009 (library bound) | ISBN 9781502618047 (ebook)
Subjects: LCSH: Civilization, Medieval—Juvenile literature.
Classification: LCC CB351.G46 2016 | DDC 940.1—dc23

For Brown Bear Books Ltd:
Editorial Director: Lindsey Lowe
Managing Editor: Tim Cooke
Children's Publisher: Anne O'Daly
Design Manager: Keith Davis
Designer: Lynne Lennon
Picture Manager: Sophie Mortimer

Picture Credits:
Front Cover: Culture Club main; Shutterstock: ilolab map.
Interior: Bibliothèque Nationale de France: 43; British Library: 35; Chengzu National Palace Museum: 20; Claude Mutafian: 32; iStock: Yamak Beyter 14, 15; Louvre Museum, Paris: 7; Mats Halldin: 11; Metropolitan Museum of Art: 6; Musée Conde: RMN 27; National Portrait Gallery: 34; Robert Hunt Library: 42; Shutterstock: Vlacheslav Lopatin 37, Artono 28, Mehmet Cetin 12, FrankfurtDave 36, Jorisvo 24, Pecoid 38, Silia Photo 10; Thinkstock: Tom Brakefield 8, Curtoicurto 22, Luhan Feng 21, gameover2012 ifc, 13, Muharremz 19, Orhan 18, Photos.com 9, 16, 17, 23, 25, 30, 31, 39, 41, Roman Sigaev 40; Topfoto: Picturepoint 29; Universitätsbibliothek Heidelberg: 26; Universtity of California: 33.

Printed in the United States of America

CONTENTS

INTRODUCTION

Primary sources are the best way to get close to people from the past. They include the things people wrote in diaries, letters, or books; the paintings, drawings, maps, or cartoons they created; and even the buildings they constructed, the clothes they wore, or the objects they owned. Such sources often reveal a lot about how people saw themselves and how they thought about their world.

This book collects a range of primary sources from the Middle Ages or medieval period. The period is only vaguely defined. As rough markers of its start and end, historians sometimes use the fall of the Roman Empire in the West in the fifth century and the capture of Constantinople by the Ottoman Turks in 1453.

The Middle Ages was a period of both change and stability. For most people, life was hard and short. Hunger and sickness were constant threats. Yet the Catholic Church inspired a revival of learning, and Europe's kings began to increase their power in ways that would lead to the emergence of modern countries. In Asia, the new religion of Islam inspired great cultural advances. Supporters of Islam, or Muslims, clashed with European Christians in a number of military conflicts known as the Crusades. The Crusades were signs that the medieval world was becoming larger and more international.

HOW TO USE THIS BOOK

Each spread contains at least one primary source. Look out for "Source Explored" boxes that explain images from the Middle Ages and who made them and why. There are also "As They Saw It" boxes that contain quotes from people of the period.

Some boxes contain more detailed information about a particular aspect of a subject. The subjects are arranged in roughly chronological order. They focus on key events or people. There is a full timeline of the period at the back of the book.

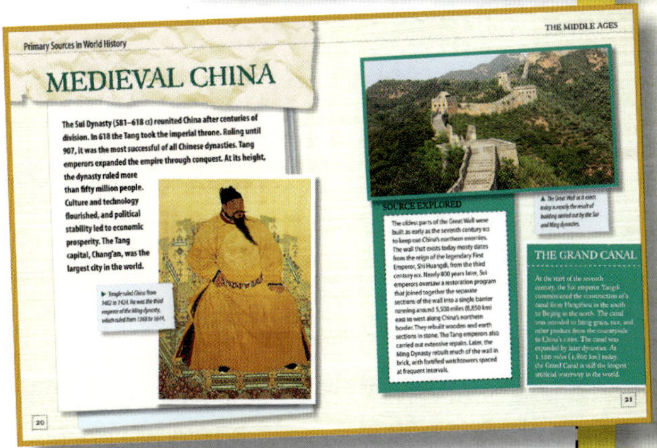

Some spreads feature a longer extract from a contemporary eyewitness. Look for the colored introduction that explains who the writer is and the origin of his or her account. These accounts are often accompanied by a related visual primary source.

MIGRATIONS OF PEOPLES

From around 375 CE, Germanic tribes known as the Visigoths and Ostrogoths moved west into the Roman Empire in central Europe. They had been pushed out of their homelands by another tribe called the Huns. The Goths and Huns were part of a movement of tribes the Romans called "barbarians," or non-Romans. These peoples moved into the disintegrating Roman Empire. Other invading barbarians included the Franks and the Vandals. These invasions weakened and ultimately destroyed the Roman Empire.

◀ These eagle-shaped earrings were created by an Ostrogoth craftsman around 500 CE. Despite Roman propaganda, many barbarian peoples had sophisticated cultures.

Ammianus Marcellinus (circa 330–395) was a Roman historian. Here he describes the Battle of Adrianople, now Edirne in Turkey, in 378 CE. The battle was the culmination of three years of warfare between the Romans and the barbarians:

"So now, with rage flashing in their eyes, the barbarians pursued our men who were in a state of torpor [physical inactivity], the warmth of their veins having deserted them. Many were slain without knowing who smote them; some were overwhelmed by the mere weight of the crowd which pressed upon them; and some were slain by wounds–inflicted by their own comrades. The barbarians spared neither those who yielded nor those who resisted. Besides these, many half-slain lay blocking up the roads, unable to endure the torture of their wounds; and heaps of dead horses were piled up and filled the plain with their carcasses [bodies]."

SOURCE EXPLORED

This bronze coin shows Attila (406–453 CE), the fierce and feared king of the Huns. The Huns were nomads from western Asia. From 434, Attila began to attack the borders of the Roman Empire. The Huns conquered large parts of eastern Europe. Attila controlled his empire from the plains of what is now Hungary. He even forced the Romans to pay him tribute, a type of payment that acknowledged Attila's authority.

◀ *Attila was one of the Romans' most feared enemies. His soldiers invaded both the Eastern and Western Roman Empires, but were unable to reach Rome itself.*

THE FALL OF ROME

In 117 CE, the Roman Empire was at its most powerful. It controlled the Mediterranean Sea, North Africa, the Middle East, and much of Europe. By 476 CE, the city of Rome itself had been captured by barbarians after a series of earlier attacks. The Roman Empire in the west had fallen. The eastern half of the empire survived, ruled from Constantinople.

▼ *The ruins of the Forum still stand in Rome. After the fall of the empire, the former capital fell into gradual disrepair.*

▲ *The marble Ludovisi Sarcophagus was discovered in 1621. It is named for its seventeenth-century owner, Cardinal Ludovisi.*

SOURCE EXPLORED

This is a detail of a carving on the side of a Roman tomb known as the Ludovisi Battle Sarcophagus. The carving shows Roman soldiers fighting the Ostrogoths, a barbarian people from Dacia in southeastern Europe. The Romans are carved in heroic poses as they beat the bearded barbarians into submission. In fact, by the time the carving was created in around 250–260 CE, the empire's borders were coming under steady barbarian attack. The superiority of the Roman troops in the carving reflects Roman propaganda rather than reality.

St. Jerome (347–420 CE) was a Roman Catholic priest and historian. Here he describes hearing news that Rome had been sacked, or attacked, by the Visigoths in 410 CE.

“A dreadful rumor came from the west. Rome had been besieged and its citizens had been forced to buy their lives with gold. Then thus despoiled they had been besieged again so as to lose not their substance only but their lives. My voice sticks in my throat; and, as I dictate, sobs choke my utterance. The city which had taken the whole world was itself taken; nay, more famine was beforehand with the sword and but few citizens were left to be made captives. In their frenzy the starving people had recourse to hideous food; and tore each other limb from limb that they might have flesh to eat. Even the mother did not spare the babe at her breast.”

THE VIKINGS

▲ *This reconstruction of a Viking longship shows its carved dragon prow and the warrior shields hanging on the sides.*

The Vikings were farmers and seafarers from what are now Sweden, Denmark, and Norway. In the eighth century these "Northmen" sailed in longships to raid coastal towns and monasteries in western Europe. From the ninth century Viking traders sailed along rivers into modern Russia and settled in eastern England and northern France. Other European kingdoms gave them land and silver in order to prevent the Vikings from attacking them. Around 1000 CE, the Viking explorer Leif Eriksson became the first European to reach North America.

▼ The Vikings often carved stones with designs or with information carved in runes, an early form of alphabet.

AS THEY SAW IT

"They came to an island which lay to the eastward of the land, and went up there and looked round them in good weather, and observed that there was dew upon the grass. And it so happened that they touched the dew with their hands, and raised the fingers to the mouth, and they thought that they had never before tasted anything so sweet."

–A Viking saga, or long story, describes Leif Eriksson's discovery of Newfoundland.

SOURCE EXPLORED

This funerary stone was carved in the eighth century CE as part of a Viking tomb. Known as the Ardre VIII stone, it is the largest of a number of funerary stones found at Ardre on the Swedish island of Gotland. The keyhole-shaped stone, which was designed to stand upright, is decorated with scenes from Norse mythology. At the top right of the stone, Odin, the chief Viking god, rides his eight-legged horse, Sleipnir, across the sky. Historians have puzzled over the other images on the stone. They might show mythological scenes such as the punishment of the trickster god, Loki, and the death of Baldr, a god of light. On the left is a longboat that resembles the ships the Vikings sailed. Important people were also sometimes buried in longboats. The stone is edged with abstract shapes that look like chain links.

THE BYZANTINE EMPIRE

Constantinople was the capital of the Eastern Roman Empire until the fall of the Western Empire in 476 CE. Constantinople, also known as Byzantium, then became the capital of the Byzantine Empire. In the sixth century, the empire grew through trade and conquest, and Byzantium became a center of culture. It was also the center of the Orthodox form of Christianity.

▼ *Later converted into a mosque, the Hagia Sophia in Byzantium was built as a Christian church by the Emperor Justinian I in the 530s.*

◀ *Accompanied by her attendants, Theodora makes an offering of a chalice to two churchmen. The chalice represents the blood of Christ.*

SOURCE EXPLORED

This mosaic was created in the Church of San Vitale in Ravenna, Italy. Ravenna had briefly been the capital of the Western Roman Empire and was the Byzantine capital of Italy. The mosaic shows the Empress Theodora (with halo) presenting a gift to two churchmen. Theodora was the wife of the Byzantine emperor Justinian, who led the empire's expansion in the sixth century. Theodora was the most important of all Byzantine empresses. Justinian relied on her advice to end a series of riots in 532 CE that threatened to overthrow his rule. Both Justinian and Theodora believed the empire was the heart of civilization and that they had a duty to preserve it. Ravenna is famous for its many mosaics, which were one of the arts that flourished under Justinian and Theodora.

AS THEY SAW IT

"The church presents a most glorious spectacle, extraordinary to those who behold it and altogether incredible... Its height rises to the very heavens and overtops the neighboring houses... It is distinguished by indescribable beauty, excelling both in size and the harmonies of its measures [proportions]."

–The historian Procopius describes the church of Hagia Sophia, finished by Justinian in Byzantium in 537.

THE SPREAD OF ISLAM

In the seventh century, a new power appeared in Arabia. Arab peoples were inspired by the teachings of the Prophet Muhammad (ca. 570–632) to adopt a new religion known as Islam. Through trade and warfare, the Arabs quickly spread Islam across a huge region from Egypt in North Africa to Iran and Iraq in Asia. Despite splits between different branches of Islam, the religion still spread. By 1450, the Muslim empire stretched from Spain in Europe to the borders of China in the east.

درجات ليبلوكم في ما آتيكم إن ربك
سريع العقاب وإنه لغفور رحيم
بسم الله الرحمن الرحيم
يس والقرآن الحكيم إنك لمن المرسلين
على صراط مستقيم تنزيل العزيز الرحيم
لتنذر قوما ما أنذر آباؤهم فهم غافلون
لقد حق القول على أكثرهم فهم لا يؤمنون إنا
جعلنا في أعناقهم أغلالا فهي إلى الأذقان فهم
مقمحون وجعلنا من بين أيديهم سدا

◀ *This is a medieval manuscript of the Koran, the holy scripture of the Islamic religion. It is decorated with gold paint, to indicate the value of its message.*

SOURCE EXPLORED

This Islamic drawing shows the mosque at Mecca in Saudi Arabia. The mosque is said to have been begun by Abraham around 2130 BCE. At its heart is the Kaaba, a black cube-shaped building that is the most sacred site in Islam. Muslims all over the world face the Kaaba when they pray. This drawing has a distinctive, one-dimensional style; following Islamic tradition, it portrays the mosque in gold. Such drawings were often created to be sold as certificates to Muslims who had made the *hajj*. This is a pilgrimage to Mecca that is the sacred duty of all Muslims who can afford the trip. Islam teaches that Muhammad was the prophet of the one god, Allah. Muhammad's teachings were unacceptable in Mecca and he fled to the rival city of Medina, but he later returned to Mecca. Islam attracted many followers with its promise of a fairer society. Later, Islam was led by caliphs who were both rulers and religious leaders. When the third caliph was murdered, Islam split into two factions, Sunni and Shia.

AS THEY SAW IT

"All those who listen to me shall pass on my words to others and those to others again; and may the last ones understand my words better than those who listen to me directly."

—The Last Sermon of Muhammad, delivered on the Ninth Day of Dhul Hijjah 10 AH (ca. 630 CE).

▶ *This painting shows the mosque in Mecca, Saudi Arabia, which is said to have been built on the site of a house built by the prophet Abraham.*

ISLAMIC CULTURE

Under a series of caliphs, or rulers, the Islamic empire developed a remarkable civilization. Islamic knowledge of science, architecture, and the arts was far greater than that of Christian Europe at the time. Islamic scholars studied ancient Greek and Egyptian works and translated them into Arabic. They used these texts as a basis on which to build their knowledge. This flowering of Islamic culture lasted some five hundred years from the eighth century under the Umayyad dynasty, first in Damascus, Syria, and later in Baghdad, Iraq.

This astrolabe was made in Persia (now Iran). Astrolabes were used to measure the height of objects in the sky above the horizon. This helped navigators calculate their latitude, or north–south position, on the globe.

SOURCE EXPLORED

This sixteenth-century Islamic miniature painting shows astronomers at the Galata Observatory in Constantinople. They are using instruments including quadrants, sextants, and astrolabes. Many of these devices were invented in the Islamic world. They were used to measure the position of the stars and planets in order to create an accurate calendar based on their movements in the sky. As well as making astronomical advances, Islamic scholars also expanded math by inventing algebra. They improved medicine, developed irrigation, and created advanced maps. They also developed a distinctive style of calligraphy and the "Arabic" numerals we still use today.

▲ *This painting of the Galata Observatory was created in 1561. The observatory had been founded by Sultan Suleiman the Magnificent in 1557.*

HOUSE OF WISDOM

The House of Wisdom was a center of scholarship founded in the ninth century in Baghdad by Caliph al-Mamoon. Scholars came from across the Islamic world to study there, including Christians and Jews. By the middle of the ninth century, the House of Wisdom had more books than any other library in the world. Scholars there studied astronomy and math. They used observation to study subjects such as medicine, zoology, and chemistry. Other specialties included geography and cartography, or mapmaking.

RISE OF THE OTTOMANS

The Islamic Ottoman Empire was founded by semi-nomadic Turkic warriors from present-day Anatolia in eastern Turkey. In 1280 the emperor Osman I began to strengthen the Ottomans' power in Turkey. In 1453, the Ottomans defeated the Byzantines and captured Constantinople, which they renamed Istanbul. From their new capital, they established an Islamic empire in much of western Asia and southeastern Europe. The empire lasted for some seven hundred years, until the end of World War I in 1918.

◀ *Ottoman builders created elaborate ceramic tiles to decorate many of their public and domestic buildings.*

In 1331, the Moroccan traveler Ibn Battuta visited Bursa, in northwestern Anatolia, just after the Ottomans had captured the city. Here he describes his impressions of the Ottoman sultan, Orhan:

> “The sultan is the greatest of the kings of the Turkmens and the richest in wealth, lands, and military forces. Of fortresses he possesses nearly a hundred, and for most of his time he is continually engaged in making the rounds of them, staying in each fortress for some days to put it into good order and examine its condition. It is said that he has never stayed for a whole month in any one town. He also fights with the infidels [Christians] continually and keeps them under siege.”

SOURCE EXPLORED

Bursa was protected by two sets of walls with five fortified gates, including this one. The city was strategically important because it lay on the Silk Road, the ancient trade route that crossed most of Asia. Under the Byzantines, Bursa was an important producer of silk. The city was first besieged by Sultan Osman I, but it was his son, Orhan, who captured the city in 1326.

▼ This gate was part of the defenses at Bursa. The city only fell after an ongoing attack lasting between six and nine years. It is not known exactly when the siege began.

MEDIEVAL CHINA

The Sui Dynasty (581–618 CE) reunited China after centuries of division. In 618 the Tang took the imperial throne. Ruling until 907, it was the most successful of all Chinese dynasties. Tang emperors expanded the empire through conquest. At its height, the dynasty ruled more than fifty million people. Culture and technology flourished, and political stability led to economic prosperity. The Tang capital, Chang'an, was the largest city in the world.

► *Yongle ruled China from 1402 to 1424. He was the third emperor of the Ming dynasty, which ruled from 1368 to 1644.*

▲ *The Great Wall as it exists today is mostly the result of building carried out by the Sui and Ming dynasties.*

SOURCE EXPLORED

The oldest parts of the Great Wall were built as early as the seventh century BCE to keep out China's northern enemies. The wall that exists today mostly dates from the reign of the legendary First Emperor, Shi Huangdi, from the third century BCE. Nearly 800 years later, Sui emperors oversaw a restoration program that joined together the separate sections of the wall into a single barrier running around 5,500 miles (8,850 km) east to west along China's northern border. They rebuilt wooden and earth sections in stone. The Tang emperors also carried out extensive repairs. Later, the Ming Dynasty rebuilt much of the wall in brick, with fortified watchtowers spaced at frequent intervals.

THE GRAND CANAL

At the start of the seventh century, the Sui emperor Yangdi commissioned the construction of a canal from Hangzhou in the south to Beijing in the north. The canal was intended to bring grain, rice, and other produce from the countryside to China's cities. The canal was expanded by later dynasties. At 1,100 miles (1,800 km) today, the Grand Canal is still the longest artificial waterway in the world.

THE CATHOLIC CHURCH

The Catholic Church was the most powerful institution in Europe, providing order after the structure of Roman authority disappeared. The Church amassed great wealth, but it also preserved learning by copying ancient texts, educated people in its churches and monasteries, founded the university system, and developed Europe's hospital system. Monks also taught agriculture and manufacturing to common people.

▼ *This cloister was built in a monastery in Tarragona in Spain. Monks used the enclosed walkway for quiet meditation.*

SOURCE EXPLORED

This miniature painting was created by the Limbourg Brothers of Holland in the fifteenth century. It shows monks fishing outside the Grande Chartreuse, the main monastery of the Carthusian religious order, in southeastern France. It shows the small red-roofed cells around the monastery walls where the monks lived in solitude and prayer. A desire to live a more spiritual life led many men and women to join monasteries and convents in the Middle Ages. The main monastic orders each had their own approach to spirituality. The Benedictines, founded in the sixth century by St. Benedict in Italy, were known for learning and education. The Cistercians put an emphasis on farming and working the land, while the Augustinians spent much of their time outside the monastery, preaching and caring for ordinary people.

▲ *This miniature painting shows the Grande Chartreuse in the foothills of the Alps.*

AS THEY SAW IT

"When you wish to sleep, they wake you, when you wish to eat, they make you fast. The night is passed praying in the church, the day in working, and there is no repose but in the refectory; and what is found there? Rotten eggs, beans with their pods on, and liquor fit for oxen."

–The thirteenth-century French monk Guyot de Provins complains about life in the Clunaic order.

THE NORMAN CONQUEST

Edward the Confessor, king of England, died in 1066. Two men claimed that the childless Edward had named them as his successor. One was Edward's cousin William, Duke of Normandy; the other was an English noble named Harold Godwinson, the Earl of Wessex. Harold took the throne, but William invaded England. He defeated Harold at Hastings on October 14, 1066. Harold was killed and William—known as the Conqueror—seized the English throne.

▼ This scene from the Bayeux Tapestry shows Norman cavalry coming ashore from their longships in England in September 1066.

King Edward (right) apparently gives Harold Godwinson a message for William of Normandy. According to the tapestry, Harold ignored the message.

SOURCE EXPLORED

This detail from the Bayeux Tapestry shows King Edward in 1064. Having no heirs, the king tells Harold Godwinson that William of Normandy will be his heir. According to the tapestry, which was most likely commissioned by William's half-brother, Bishop Odo of Bayeux, Harold later ignored the message. The "tapestry" is actually a 230-foot (70 m) long embroidery that tells the story of the invasion of England. It is propaganda in support of the Norman claim to the English throne. William introduced a French-speaking aristocracy to England. These lords built castles to show their power. He replaced most English bishops with French bishops and encouraged French traders to settle in England.

AS THEY SAW IT

"But among other things is not to be forgotten that good peace that he [William] made in this land; so that a man of any account might go over his kingdom unhurt with his bosom full of gold. No man durst slay another, had he never so much evil done to the other... He truly reigned over England."

—Extract from the Anglo-Saxon Chronicle, records of events from the ninth to the twelfth centuries.

THE FEUDAL SYSTEM

The feudal system is a social system based on rights and duties that was developed in the eighth century. In medieval Europe, all land belonged to a king or ruler, and the church. The ruler gave land to his lords and nobles in return for their loyalty. The lords and nobles gave land to their own followers. In exchange for the land, on which they grew crops, peasants were obliged to work for their lords. In turn, the lords had a duty to protect their peasants.

This illustration from an early fourteenth-century German manuscript shows nobles jousting. This "sport" helped nobles train for military action in the service of their feudal lord, the king.

▼ *This image is from a series known as the* Très Riches Heures, *which showed each month of the year. It was painted by the Limbourg brothers in 1409.*

AS THEY SAW IT

"He who swears fealty [loyalty] to his lord ... should faithfully counsel and aid his lord, if he wishes to be looked upon as worthy of his benefice [the grant of a landed estate] and to be safe concerning the fealty which he has sworn."

—Fulbert, the bishop of Chartres and the most famous scholar of his time, writes to William, Duke of Aquitaine, in around 1025 about the duties of a noble to his king.

SOURCE EXPLORED

This detail from a French illuminated manuscript from the early fifteenth century shows peasants working in the fields in October. One man uses a horse to pull a harrow to till the land while another man sows seed. The royal palace, the Louvre, is seen in the background. The feudal system was a complex system of duties and rewards. In exchange for land and protection, peasants worked an agreed number of days for their lord and also gave him a share of their produce. In turn, their lords were obliged to serve the king by providing military service for a certain number of days a year and by attending the king's court. They also had to contribute to the king's expenses. In return, the king granted them land to treat as their own. Only the king had no feudal obligations.

THE SHAPE OF CHRISTENDOM

▲ *This statue of Emperor Otto I stands in the German town of Magdeburg. Otto's rule brought together many small states throughout the heart of Europe.*

In the tenth and eleventh centuries the map of Europe was different from today. Europe itself was known as Christendom—the place where Christians lived. Modern countries were emerging in England and France, but elsewhere the continent was divided into small states. In 962, the Pope crowned Otto I of Germany as Holy Roman Emperor. Otto ruled a vast territory including the Low Countries and present-day Germany and Italy.

The crown of the Holy Roman Emperor was unusual. It was made up of eight separate panels that were joined by hinges.

SOURCE EXPLORED

This jewel-encrusted crown was used in the coronation of Otto I as King of the Romans, the title given to the Holy Roman Emperor. The crown was used by all the rulers until the dissolution of the Holy Roman Empire in 1806. It is made of gold set with 144 precious stones and small enamel panels showing scenes from the Bible. The magnificence of the crown reinforced the power of the Holy Roman Emperor, who was appointed by the Pope as "defender of the faith." The empire's name was intended to echo the glory of the ancient Roman Empire. Although Europe's kings held earthly power, spiritual power remained with the Catholic Church. This caused difficult choices for nobles when the wishes of the monarch and those of the church were opposed to each other.

AS THEY SAW IT

"It has the color of wine, of delicate red wine and it is as if the dazzling white of snow penetrates the bright wine red and yet it remains dormant in this redness. The gem shines powerfully and it is said that it once even shone at night, but not in our time, but it is said to preserve the honor of the empire."

–The scholar Albert the Great describes the "Orphan," a large jewel now missing from the imperial crown, in 1250.

THE CRUSADES

In 1095, Pope Urban II called on Christians to liberate the holy city of Jerusalem, which had been conquered by the Islamic Empire in 637. In return, Urban promised forgiveness of their sins. Over the next two centuries, many thousands of Christian soldiers traveled to the Holy Land (Palestine) to fight in a series of nine separate crusades. They conquered Jerusalem and set up small Crusader states, but they fought among themselves and the Muslims took back control of the Holy Land by about 1300.

◀ *This French illustration from 1244 shows the crusaders capturing the port city of Acre during the Third Crusade in 1191.*

SOURCE EXPLORED

This illustration shows a battle from the First Crusade (1096–1099) as imagined by the French artist Sebastian Marmoret four hundred years later. The first Crusader armies were largely untrained peasants and religious fanatics who were massacred by Muslim troops. The Frankish knights who followed were more effective and captured Jerusalem after a siege. The Crusaders set up their own states in the Holy Land. They soon fell out among themselves, however. In 1204, during the Fourth Crusade, Crusaders destroyed Constantinople, even though the Byzantines were fellow Christians. That prevented any reconciliation between the Catholic and Orthodox branches of Christianity. Two orders of warrior monks, the Hospitallers and the Templars, were the elite of the Crusaders' religious military forces.

▲ *The French artist Sebastian Marmoret depicts close-range hand-to-hand fighting.*

AS THEY SAW IT

"If you wish to be mindful of your souls, advance boldly, as knights of Christ, and rush as quickly as you can to the defense of the Eastern Church. Under Jesus Christ, our Leader, may you struggle for your Jerusalem, in Christian battle line ... that you may assail and drive out the Turks ... And may you deem it a beautiful thing to die for Christ in that city in which He died for us."

–Pope Urban II summons the knights of Europe to the First Crusade, 1095.

THE MONGOL INVASIONS

The Mongols were nomadic horsemen from central Asia who became a formidable force under their ruler, Genghis Khan (ca.1162–1227). Under Genghis and his descendents, including his grandsons Kublai and Hulagu, the Mongols used their outstanding skills as cavalry warriors to conquer a huge empire that stretched from China to eastern Europe. The empire was divided into khanates, or states, which broke apart after 1259. The states included the Golden Horde, which was based in modern Russia, and the Ilkhanate in what are now Iran and its neighbors.

◀ *In this miniature painting, Ghazan, the ruler of the Ilkhanate, converts to Islam on coming to the throne in 1295.*

SOURCE EXPLORED

This Persian illustration shows Hulagu's Mongol warriors besieging the city of Baghdad in 1258. The city was the capital of the Abbasid caliphate. It was protected by two walls and a moat with a drawbridge. Outside, Mongol archers stand beside a giant catapult for throwing missiles at the city walls. After a twelve-day siege, the city surrendered. In retaliation for the city's initial resistance, the Mongol warriors destroyed the city and massacred at least ninety thousand of its citizens. The defeat brought an end to the golden age of Islamic culture that had flowered in Baghdad under the Abbasids.

▲ Islamic defenders fire arrows from the walls of Baghdad at the Mongol besiegers.

The Persian writer Juvayni wrote *The History of the World Conqueror* in 1260, about the rise of Genghis Khan:

> "And in those days the Mongol tribes were not united and did not obey one another. When Genghis Khan rose from the grade of childhood to the degree of manhood, he became in the onslaught like a roaring lion and in the melee like a trenchant sword; in the subjugation of his foes his rigor and severity had the taste of poison, and in the humbling of the pride of each lord of fortune his harshness and ferocity did the work of Fate ... Day by day he raised his station and position, until all affairs of state were dependent upon him."

KINGS AND PARLIAMENTS

Monarchs were at the heart of Europe's kingdoms. A king's strength depended on his ability to command loyalty from his nobles, rather than on any fixed borders. Kings maintained splendid courts as a means to show their superiority over their nobles. In order to maintain power, a king needed the support of his barons. From the thirteenth century, some monarchs set up parliaments, organizations formed by nobles, to approve the king's ideas.

◀ This fourteenth-century painting shows King John of England hunting with dogs. John's harsh rule and his expensive overseas wars made him very unpopular with the English.

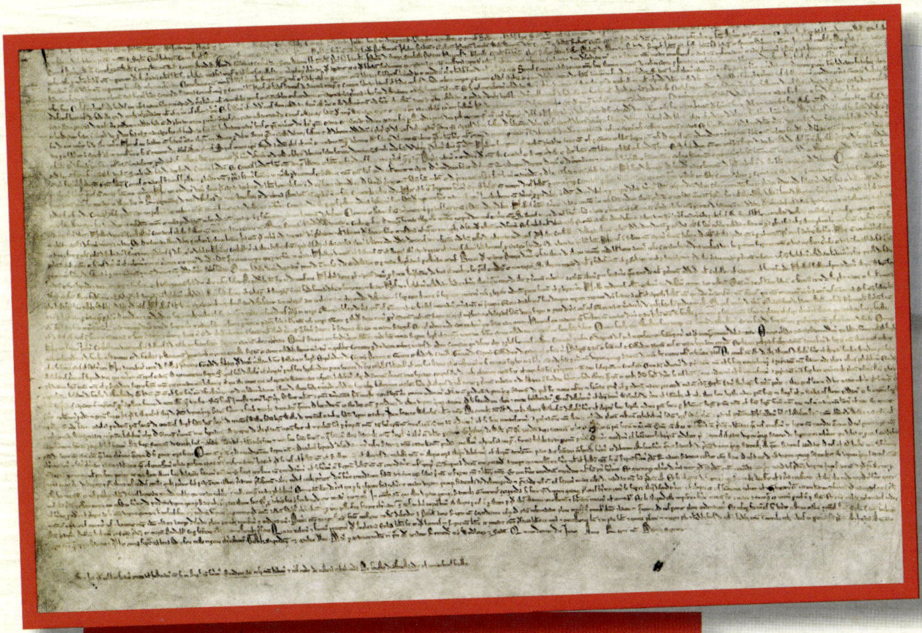

Copies of Magna Carta were sent out to nobles throughout England. No one knows how many copies were made. Today, only four survive.

SOURCE EXPLORED

This is the first page of the Magna Carta, or "Great Charter." On June 15, 1215, English barons forced King John to sign the charter at Runnymede in England. John was unpopular among his barons, from whom he had tried to raise taxes to pay for wars against France. Written on parchment in Latin, the charter set limits on how much tax John could demand from them. It also stopped him from punishing any subject without first holding a trial in a court of law. The document marked a great historical moment. It was the first time an English king had been made subject to the rule of law. Previously, the king could act however he chose. From 1215 onward, he needed the approval of his barons.

AS THEY SAW IT

"It is called Magna Carta ... in respect of the great importance, and weightinesse of the matter.... It was for the most part declatory of the principall grounds of the fundamentall laws of England."

—Sir Edward Coke, English chief justice, attorney general, and member of parliament, ca. 1628.

BUILDING THE CATHEDRALS

From about the mid-eleventh century, cathedrals were built throughout countries such as England, France, and what is now Germany. A magnificent cathedral was a sign of a town's importance. Its spire could be seen from miles away. Building work took decades or sometimes centuries to complete. Construction was a community effort and involved many craftspeople. The decoration of a cathedral helped to teach Christian stories to illiterate worshipers.

◀ *Construction of Salisbury Cathedral in England took from 1220 to 1320, although the main part of the building was finished by 1258.*

In 1220 an English bishop wrote a long Latin poem entitled the "Metrical Life of St. Hugh." In it, the bishop explains the use of symbols in Lincoln Cathedral, England:

> "The foundation is the body, the wall is the man, the roof is the spirit; the division of the church is thus threefold ... Illuminating the world with heavenly light is the distinguished band of the clergy, and this is expressed by the bright windows ... The twin windows that offer a circular light are the two eyes of the cathedral; and rightly the greater of these is seen to be the bishop and the lesser the dean. For north represents the devil, and south the Holy Spirit and it is in these directions that the two Eyes look.... With these Eyes the cathedral's face is on the watch for the candelabra of heaven..."

SOURCE EXPLORED

Construction of the cathedral of Notre Dame in Paris, France, started in 1163. It was built in a completely new type of architecture now called the Gothic style. It had large, circular, stained-glass windows that flooded the interior with light. The building had huge stone walls and a ceiling that was 115 feet (35 m) above the floor. Such a high ceiling was made possible by the use of "flying buttresses." These huge arched stone supports on the outside of the building helped hold up the weight of the roof.

▲ *Notre Dame was finally opened in 1345, 182 years after construction began. Today it is one of the most famous churches in the world.*

PILGRIMAGE

▲ *Christians believe the remains of St. James the Apostle are held at Santiago de Compostella in northwest Spain.*

An important rite for many Christians was the pilgrimage. This was a special journey to a holy place or shrine. The church taught that making a pilgrimage would earn Christ's forgiveness for any sins. All types of people made long journeys on foot or horseback to cathedrals where relics of famous saints were kept. One important shrine was that of St. James the Apostle in Santiago de Compostella in northern Spain. Four main pilgrim routes to his shrine led across France and Spain.

SOURCE EXPLORED

This is a page from a fourteenth-century manuscript of a long English poem entitled *The Canterbury Tales*. It shows the poet, Geoffrey Chaucer (ca. 1343–1400), dressed as a pilgrim on a horse. Pilgrims usually traveled in groups for protection and companionship. Chaucer's poem describes a group of pilgrims on their way from London to the shrine of St. Thomas Becket in Canterbury, England. The pilgrims tell each other stories to help pass the time. The journey to Canterbury took around three to five days, but other pilgrimages could take months. Pilgrims wore badges to identify themselves, and carried wooden sticks for protection. They often made the last part of the journey barefooted to show they were humble. Along the route, there was a network of inns or monasteries where pilgrims could eat and rest overnight.

▲ *This image of Geoffrey Chaucer comes from a 240-page manuscript of* The Canterbury Tales.

AS THEY SAW IT

“Pilgrims, whether poor or rich, returning from St. James or going there must be received with charity and compassion; for those whosoever receives them and gives them hospitality has for his guest not only St. James but our Lord Himself.”

–The Pilgrim's Guide: A Twelfth-Century Guide for the Pilgrim to St. James of Compostella, ca. 1140–1150.

THE BLACK DEATH

The Black Death struck Europe in 1347. It was a plague spread by fleas on black rats carried on ships from Asia. The plague was highly contagious and killed sufferers within days. For six years, the plague spread through Europe. It killed about 33 percent of the population—about twenty-five million people. Such losses had a huge impact on society. There was a shortage of workers, for example, so those who survived were able to travel and ask for higher wages.

During the Black Death, so many people died that their bones were stored in special chambers known as ossuaries.

Although the Catholic Church condemned the practice of flagellation, it remained popular during the Black Death.

SOURCE EXPLORED

This painting from a 1349 manuscript shows a group of flagellants in the Netherlands. Flagellants were extreme Christians who whipped themselves as a form of penance. They believed the Black Death was God's way of punishing humanity for their sins. They thought harming themselves would earn God's forgiveness. Other people reacted to the plague by spending their time thinking about the end of the world. So many people died during the plague that they were buried in huge pits because there were not enough coffins. In Paris alone, almost eight hundred people died every day. Many people blamed "outsiders" for causing the plague by poisoning water in wells. They attacked groups such as Jews, the sick, or Muslims in order to punish them.

AS THEY SAW IT

"The violence of this disease was such that the sick communicated it to the healthy who came near them, just as a fire catches anything dry or oily near it. And it even went further. To speak to or go near the sick brought infection and a common death to the living; and moreover, to touch the clothes or anything else the sick had touched or worn gave the disease to the person touching."

—The Italian writer Giovanni Boccaccio, who survived the plague in 1348, describes how deadly it was.

THE HUNDRED YEARS' WAR

What is called the Hundred Years' War actually lasted nearly 120 years. From 1337 to 1453, the Plantagenet dynasty of England fought intermittently with the French House of Valois for control of Plantagenet lands in France. The war lasted for five generations of ruler on either side. Despite famous English victories at Crécy (1346), Poitiers (1356), and Agincourt (1415), France emerged as the ultimate victor. The victory was a key step in the creation of the French nation state.

This 1505 illustration shows Joan of Arc. The peasant girl became a French heroine after helping to break the English siege of the city of Orléans in 1429. She was executed by the English in May 1431.

SOURCE EXPLORED

This fifteenth-century painting shows the French (*left*) and English forces at the Battle of Crécy, fought on August 26, 1346, in northern France. Led by King Edward III (ruled 1327–1377), the English defeated a far larger French army led by King Philip VI (ruled 1328–1350). The English used the new longbow, which had a longer range than the French crossbows, allowing the English archers to rain down arrows on the enemy. The English also used very early cannon in the battle. The victory of the English infantry has been seen as marking the end of the dominance of the mounted knight in battle. Victory at Crécy allowed the English to protect the port they held on the French coast at Calais. Calais remained in English hands until 1558.

▲ *This detail is taken from an illustrated manuscript of Jean Froissart's* Chronicles, *created in the 1470s.*

AS THEY SAW IT

“[This Voice] ... said to me two or three times a week: 'You must go into France.' It said to me: 'Go, raise the siege which is being made before the City of Orléans. Go!' it added, 'to Robert de Baudricourt, Captain of Vaucouleurs: he will furnish you with an escort to accompany you.' And I replied that I was but a poor girl, who knew nothing of riding or fighting.”

–Joan of Arc led French troops at the Siege of Orleans in 1429, which led to the final French victory. Joan claimed to be guided by voices from God.

TIMELINE

476	*Fall of the Roman Empire in the West with the capture of Rome by the barbarian leader, Odoacer, who became King of Italy.*
570	*Birth of Muhammad, founder of Islam.*
609	*The Grand Canal is completed in China.*
618	*The Tang Dynasty comes to the imperial throne in China.*
637	*As Islam spreads, Arab warriors capture Jerusalem.*
732	*The Franks defeat a Muslim army in the Battle of Tours, preventing a Muslim invasion of Europe.*
793	*Scandinavian Vikings attack Lindisfarne Monastery off the northeast coast of England; this is the first of a series of raids of coastal settlements in northern Europe that continue until 1042.*
800	*Charlemagne, the king of the Franks of what is now France, is crowned as the first Holy Roman Emperor, unifying much of western Europe.*
862	*Vikings form a state in Russia, first at Novgorod, later at Kiev.*
871	*Alfred the Great becomes the first king of a united England.*
907	*End of the Tang Dynasty in China.*
910	*An abbey is founded at Cluny in France; it becomes the center of the monastic movement in Europe.*
962	*Otto of Germany is crowned Holy Roman Emperor.*
ca.1000	*The Viking seafarer Leif Eriksson lands in North America.*
1054	*The Christian Church splits into the Catholic Church and the Eastern Orthodox, or Byzantine, Church.*
1066	*WIlliam, Duke of Normandy, defeats King Harold of England in the Battle of Hastings and claims the throne; he introduces a Norman aristocracy to run the state in England.*
1085	*William the Conqueror commissions a great survey of his kingdom, later known as the Domesday Book.*
1095	*In response to a summons from Pope Urban II to help the Byzantine Christians regain control over Christian sites in the Holy Land, Europeans set out on the First Crusade; there will be more crusades over the following two hundred years.*

1147	*The Second Crusade begins after Muslims conquer the Crusader state of Edessa; the crusade is a failure.*
1163	*Construction begins on the cathedral of Notre Dame in Paris.*
1189	*After Saladin recaptures Jerusalem in 1187, the Third Crusade begins. It fails to reclaim Jerusalem.*
1204	*During the Fourth Crusade, European soldiers capture the Byzantine capital at Constantinople.*
1206	*Genghis Khan is elected king of the Mongols and founds the Mongol Empire.*
1215	*King John of England signs the Magna Carta, or Great Charter, which gives his barons some control over his actions and recognizes that a monarch is not above the law.*
1258	*The Mongols besiege and capture Baghdad, ending the golden age of Islamic culture.*
1272	*The Ninth Crusade begins; it is generally seen as the last of Europe's Crusades against the Muslims.*
1299	*Osman I founds the Ottoman Empire.*
1337	*The Hundred Years' War breaks out between England and France over control of English territory in France.*
1346	***August 26:** English forces defeat a larger French force in the Battle of Crécy, thanks in part to the English longbows.*
1347	*The Black Death arrives in Europe.*
1415	***October 25:** The English army of Henry V inflicts a devastating defeat on the French in the Battle of Agincourt.*
1429	*Claiming to be guided by God, Joan of Arc helps the French lift the siege of Orléans by the English, allowing the coronation of Charles VII of France.*
1431	***May 30:** Joan of Arc is executed by the English.*
1439	*Johannes Gutenberg invents the printing press in Europe; it will be a major factor in the spread of the Renaissance.*
1453	*The Ottoman Turks conquer Constantinople, ending the Byzantine Empire.* *The Hundred Years' War ends in defeat for England, although it held on to the port of Calais in France until 1558.*

GLOSSARY

absolution Forgiveness for one's sins.

aristocracy A high social class of people of noble birth.

astrolabe An instrument for making astronomical measurements.

barbarians The name given by the Romans to peoples who lived outside their empire.

caliph The main Muslim ruler and spiritual leader, who was seen as the successor of Muhammad.

Christendom The name used for the Christian region of Europe in the Middle Ages.

dissolution The formal ending of an official body.

dynasty A series of rulers who all come from the same family.

feudal Describes a political system in which all land is held in return for service to a monarch or lord.

funerary Relating to a tomb.

Gothic A style of architecture noted for pointed arches and large windows.

illiterate Unable to read.

illumination A colored design or painting in an old manuscript.

longbow A tall bow used by English archers from the fourteenth century.

longship A long, narrow warship powered by oars or by a square sail.

manuscript A book or document written by hand.

miniature A small, highly detailed, painting.

monastic orders Societies of monks or nuns who live according to particular rules.

mosaic A picture created from small pieces of glass, tile, or stone.

mosque A building for Islamic worship.

nomads People who move around and have no fixed homes.

Orthodox Belonging to the Greek Orthodox Church.

parchment A prepared animal skin used as a surface for writing.

penance A punishment undertaken to show regret for a sin.

plague A highly contagious disease that causes fever, delirium, and death.

propaganda Material designed to support a particular point of view.

saga A long Viking story that describes a heroic achievement.

sarcophagus An ancient stone coffin with carved surfaces.

shrine A place seen as holy because of its connection to a god, sacred person, or relic.

siege A military operation in which a location is surrounded and forced to surrender.

tribute Payment made by one state or ruler to another, usually as a sign of the other's seniority.

FURTHER INFORMATION

Books

Allen, Kathy. *The Horrible, Miserable Middle Ages*. Mankato, MN: Capstone Press, 2010.

Davenport, John. *The Age of Feudalism*. World History. Detroit: Lucent Books, 2007.

Hattstein, Markus, and Hermann-Josef Udelhoven. *The Middle Ages and the Early Modern Period*. Witness to History. New York: Rosen Publishing Group, 2012.

Jeffrey, Gary, and Terry Riley. *The Crusades*. Graphic Medieval History. New York: Crabtree Publishing Company, 2014.

Langley, Andrew. *Medieval Life*. Eyewitness Books. New York: DK Eyewitness Books, 2011.

Matten, Joanne. *Medieval Times: England in the Middle Ages*. Primary Source Readers: World History. Teacher Created Materials, 2013.

Slavicek, Louise Chipley. *The Black Death*. Great Historic Disasters. New York. Chelsea House Publications, 2008.

Trembinski, Donna. *Famous People of the Middle Ages*. Medieval World. Crabtree Publishing Co, 2006.

Websites

www.bbc.co.uk/history/british/
A BBC website about the Norman conquest of England and its results.

www.eyewitnesstohistory.com/mefrm.htm
Eyewitness accounts of key episodes from the Middle Ages and the Renaissance.

www.history.com/topics/middle-ages
An overview of the Middle Ages from History.com, with links and videos.

www.themiddleages.net/
A gateway with links to pages about many aspects of medieval life.renni

Publisher's note to educators and parents: Our editors have carefully reviewed these websites to ensure that they are suitable for students. Many websites change frequently, however, and we cannot guarantee that a site's future contents will continue to meet our high standards of quality and educational value. Be advised that students should be closely supervised whenever they access the Internet.

INDEX